STRATHCLYDE UNIVERSITY LIBRARY

30125 00076413 3

KV-038-817

ANDERSONIAN LIBRARY
★
DRAWN
M
LIBRARY
STOCK
★
UNIVERSITY OF STRATHCLYDE

UNIVERSITY OF
STRATHCLYDE LIBRARIES

Heavy Goods Vehicles

1919-1939

by

Nick Baldwin

ALMARK

Almark Publishing Co. Ltd., London

© 1976 Almark Publishing Co. Ltd.
Text © Nick Baldwin

All rights reserved. No part of this publication may be
reproduced, stored in a retrieval system or transmitted
by any means electronic, mechanical, or by photocopying,
without prior permission of the publishers.

First Published 1976.

ISBN 0 85524 266 3

FLOOD DAMAGE
2 0 JAN 1996

Printed in Great Britain by
Chapel River Press,
Andover, Hants.
for the publishers, Almark Publishing Co. Ltd.
49 Malden Way, New Malden,
Surrey KT3 6EA, England.

D
629.22409204·2
HEA

D
629.22409
BAL

CONTENTS

INTRODUCTION

The twenty years between the two World Wars saw the most enormous changes, not least in road transport.

Cars during the period were improved and modernised, but most contained recognisably similar features whether made in 1919 or 1939. On the other hand, heavy goods vehicles were completely transformed in the same twenty years. From the lumbering load carriers that would not have looked out of place in late Victorian steam engineering days, they emerged as light-weight, speedy, technically advanced, purpose-built vehicles with a motive power that had not even been tried at the start of the period. Not only did they have diesel engines but also they had acquired pneumatic tyres, all wheel servo brakes, enclosed cabs, multi axles, electric in place of oil and acetylene lighting, and countless other innovations. This had not only transformed their appearance but had helped them to challenge the railways' virtual monopoly of goods haulage.

In tracing the development of 3 ton and upwards commercial vehicles during the period, I have leant heavily on the comprehensive photographic and historic records owned by the *Old Motor* magazine in London. These have been invaluable and I express my appreciation to Prince Marshall, the managing editor. My thanks also to Arthur Ingram for use of his remarkable collection of historic transport material, and to John Smith for his help in selecting and copying photographs. Finally I am very grateful to the various manufacturers and operators, notably British Oil Ltd, who have helped to find photographs of some of the most elusive types of vehicle.

1087

Like the R.A.F.-type Leyland there were still plenty of World War I AEC Y types in service in 1930. However, they were beginning to require expensive engine attention so a logical step was the installation of one of the new diesels. Here a five cylinder L2 Gardner has been squeezed into the space formerly occupied by a smaller four cylinder petrol engine.

Heavy Goods Vehicles 1919-1939

World War I provided an incentive for traditional truck manufacturers to increase their production, and for countless servicemen to learn about the mysteries of driving and maintaining motor vehicles for the first time.

When the war ended it was natural for many of these drivers returning to civilian life to decide that their future lay in road transport. They started motor repair, car hire, and petrol storage garages, became shoestring motor manufacturers catering for the expected boom in cheap light cars, or else bought a lorry and set to work as haulage contractors.

For a short time in 1919, the demand for lorries led to a boom in the motor factories where there was no need to design anything more modern than the solid tyred and often chain driven 3 to 4 tonners that they had been supplying to the War Department since 1914. However, by 1920, the heavy vehicle market had become saturated because a slump had rapidly replaced the early peace time trade boom, and there were too many hauliers chasing too few haulage contracts. To add to the manufacturers' difficulties, the War Department started to release its enormous fleet of war surplus vehicles, and soon thousands of lorries were changing hands in auction sales around the country for less than half the price of comparable new vehicles. Many of these machines were late deliveries, so had seen little or no service and were naturally an attractive purchase, in many cases the equal of the lorries still emerging from the factories.

Admittedly some ex-WD vehicles were better than others, so hauliers who had selected unsatisfactory makes, or were unlucky with their particular models, were soon driven out of business, leaving the field open to the others to expand from one man operations into fleets. The choice of vehicle was important, and wartime Leyland, AEC, Dennis, Thornycroft and Albion (all of whom had supplied 5,000-10,000 WD lorries), and other smaller makes, like Commer, Daimler and Maudslay, were soon the basis of many successful fleets. There were, however, those who preferred the American lorries left behind by the U.S. army or supplied to Allied governments. These far outnumbered the British made vehicles and included some excellent models from companies like Mack, Packard, Peerless, Pierce-Arrow and FWD. Two of these makes in particular were to leave their mark on British haulage. One was the Peerless, which continued to be reconditioned at Slough for many years and finally became an all-British vehicle when supplies of American parts ran out. The other was the FWD. This and the Nash or Jeffery Quad were the first four wheel drive lorries to be seen in Britain, and the FWD especially soon earned a good reputation in heavy haulage and off-road tipping work. It too was reconditioned and rebuilt at Slough, close to the vast government vehicle disposal depot. Following AEC interest in the company from 1929, the two firms collaborated on the famous four and six wheel drive AECs of the late Thirties and war years.

Of the British vehicles, perhaps the one to earn the highest reputation was the R.A.F. type Leyland 3 to 4 tonner. This was partly due to it being a basically sound design and partly due to the manufacturer's policy of carrying out their own reconditioning work to the surviving 3,000, rather than letting them get into the hands of possibly unscrupulous dealers. The result was a higher priced vehicle than the typical reconditioned WD 3 tonner, but at least it had a guarantee, and operators knew that any suspect parts would always have been replaced. These continued to be supplied by Leyland until 1926, when stocks finally ran out. Incidentally, the 3 ton capacity was by far the most numerous of the heavy vehicles of the time because this was the pre-war payload requirement that the Ministry of Munitions had published in a standard specification for the type of vehicles they needed. Lorries which complied with this Subsidy Scheme were bought before the war by civilian operators who were then paid a fee for keeping them in fit condition for call-up.

Despite the 3 ton classification, they were in fact very strongly built and were frequently called upon to carry 6 tons and more in the cut-throat transport world of the Twenties.

As we have seen, broadly similar vehicles to those produced for Subsidy requirements continued to trickle from the manufacturers after the war and, with the slump in demand, few could afford to develop new heavy models until the mid Twenties. Indeed, the ageing chain drive RC Commer continued until 1928. Although, with the exception of Albion and Scammell and the various steam wagons, most of the other immediate post-war heavy models had shaft drive, they were all broadly similar in other respects, with open sided and often windscreenless cabs, solid tyres, primitive pair-cast four cylinder engines seldom capable of more than 1300 rpm, separately mounted three or four speed crash gearboxes, and two wheel brakes, aided by a transmission brake. They seldom developed more than 50 bhp, and their leisurely performance and inadequate stopping power made the 12 mph speed limit imposed on them a highly sensible and desirable restriction. Some steam lorries with steel tyres were compelled to travel even more slowly.

Not surprisingly, the mid Twenties saw the end of most of the waggon manufacturers whose products had not evolved from the traditional horizontal boilered overtype layout. True, the well made products from Foden continued to appeal to traditionalists into the Thirties, but in general steam's last stand was confined to the tiny manufacturers who could weather the storm because of their minimal sales and low overheads, even at the best of times, and to the very advanced makers of undertype waggons like Sentinel, who were still able to sell a few vehicles right up to World War II. To put the steam waggon into perspective, of 342,920 goods vehicles on Great Britain's roads in 1930 only 7,750 were steam powered.

However, the days of the steam lorry were numbered from the moment in 1928 that solid-tyred vehicles were penalised by extra road duty and restricted to 12 mph at a time when the legal speed of their pneumatic-tyred sisters was increased to 20 mph. This was a blow to the old petrol vehicles as well, though those with a useful life expectancy were often converted to pneumatics. It was frequently impossible to modify old steamers on account of their high weight, and because of recent legislation in 1926 demanding extra mechanical as opposed to engine braking. The 1928 legislation was not as unfair as at first apparent because solids had been found to be far more damaging to road surfaces than the newly introduced giant pneumatics. After the end of 1932 all new haulage vehicles were compelled to have pneumatic tyres, and those still in use with solids were given until 1940 to change.

The early Twenties saw gradual refinement to existing petrol engined lorry designs, and the more scientific use of modern materials allowed typical payloads to increase to 6 or 7 tons; however the unladen weight stayed much the same as the old over-built 3 tonners with their equal depth girder chassis and unnecessarily heavy castings. This also helped to oust the steamer, which had previously had the 5 ton and upwards class more or less to itself, and which had been particularly popular for drawbar trailer work.

The Scammell design was largely responsible for the advance of the petrol engine into the 10 to 12 ton market, while high quality heavy rigid petrol-engined vehicles like the Saurer, often used for heavy drawbar trailer work, brought the advantages of pneumatic tyres to the 6 ton solo class as early as 1925. To operators' surprise, these expensive tyres had turned out to last longer than solids and, because of reduced rolling resistance, had also helped to improve fuel consumption from the typical 5-6 mpg of the old 3 tonner to more like 8 mpg on the new 6 ton four wheelers.

The Saurer also introduced another feature to Britain from its cold homeland of Switzerland, the enclosed cab. British vehicles had been gradually becoming less spartan with the arrival of the glass windscreen in the early Twenties in place of the traditional wind dodger, a canvas shroud that filled the cab sides and buckled to the back of the cab at neck level. At the same time, side doors were fitted, and it was only a short step from there in the late

Goods Vehicles on the Roads of Great Britain in 1930 and 1935

The table below illustrates the dramatic arrival of the diesel engine to heavy road transport and the decline of steam. Figures for electric, agricultural and showmen's vehicles were listed separately and are not included. Records were kept of vehicles by unladen weight, in this case roughly corresponding to 3 to 8 ton four wheelers in the first three lines down Column A and 10 to 15 ton six and eight wheelers in the over 5 ton unladen weight category at the bottom of Column A.

1930			Column A	1935				
Internal combustion engine*	Steam	Percentage of all goods vehicles on roads**	Unladen weight in tons	Internal combustion engine	Steam	Coal Gas	Diesel	Percentage of all goods vehicles on roads**
10,454	5	3	2½-3	16,143	3	1	254	4
22,316	50	7	3-4	16,654	12	1	1,042	4
22,104	1,168	7	4-5	13,482	76	3	1,600	4
5,107	6,515	3	Over 5	5,856	1,871	2	1,801	2

* Virtually all petrol engines with very few diesels, mainly Mercedes-Benz and Saurer.
** These figures are rounded up to the nearest whole number. The other '80 per cent' and '86 per cent' respectively in this table were all vehicles under 2½ tons.

Source: Ministry of Transport Census 1935

Twenties to fill in the gap between the top of the doors and the cab roof with glass to make them fully wind and water proof. Light vehicles had, from the early Twenties, gained the benefit of this luxury, particularly on the American imports. These tended to be produced in such large quantities that it paid the manufacturers to tool up for pressed steel cabs in place of the traditional wooden coach built variety. Unfortunately, the far lower sales volumes of heavier British lorries made modern cabs impractical, and even in the Thirties the majority were wooden framed, though metal clad.

Another mid Twenties development was forward control; this produced extra body space to cab space ratio for a given wheelbase. It was by no means a new idea, having been available on many vehicles in Edwardian days, though soon neglected when the extra engine accessibility of normal control had been endorsed by the War Department. Another scheme to have been toyed with long before was articulated vehicles, but in 1923 these received new impetus when it was realised that a superimposed trailer would allow a normal rigid goods vehicle to carry perhaps twice as much as originally envisaged. Scammell were quick to take advantage of this legal concession which allowed for a gross weight of up to 22 tons, and they made a speciality of 'artics' for many years.

An alternate way of getting the greatest possible payload was the six wheel rigid vehicle, and it is surprising that this did not appear in Britain before 1923. After all, it was a comparatively simple matter to tag on a third axle, especially if it was a trailing as opposed to a driven type. Caledon were probably the first to made a rigid six goods model in Britain in 1924, though several other firms like Maudslay, Thornycroft and Karrier were experimenting at the time. As this was a new class of vehicle not catered for in law it was for some years regarded legally as an artic. Despite the obvious payload advantages of having a rigid six, it suffered from solid rubber tyre scrub on corners, and it was not widely adopted for heavy goods haulage in the maximum 10 to 12 ton payload class, except by Sentinel and Foden steamers, until suitable pneumatic tyres became available in the late Twenties. Most of the earlier six wheelers, notably from Leyland after 1925, were for lower payloads, and they were used extensively by the services and in Britain's colonies, where both rear axles were driven. However these vehicles hardly come into the story of British goods haulage, though a similar Subsidy Scheme to World War I 3 tonners applied. These WD pattern rigid sixes were made by Guy, Thornycroft, Albion, Crossley, Morris, Vulcan, Karrier, Leyland and others, and were primarily given three axles to improve off-road traction. Both Guy and Karrier made a speciality of six wheelers, and in the late Twenties produced both passenger and haulage models so equipped. Nearly all the other big manufacturers offered 10 to 12 ton rigid sixes from 1929/30.

Cars and light commercial vehicles had been fitted with all wheel, as opposed to only rear wheel, brakes since 1923, and these gradually spread to the heavier categories during the Twenties. During the Thirties, multi-wheelers mostly received brakes on all axles, whilst a better understanding of the need for the engine to be working at optimum revs for both power and fuel consumption led to the adoption of extra gear ratios from the late Twenties. Five and six speed gearboxes became commonplace, though traditional four speed units with dual ratio auxiliary boxes to multiply the available number of gears were preferred by some manufacturers and operators.

The Twenties also saw a number of fundamental changes to the engines of goods vehicles. Except for special high speed purposes, as for fire engines and for luxury passenger travel, four cylinders had always been adequate. After all, they provided the moderate power outputs sufficient for low speed goods haulage, and were believed to give better fuel consumption than six cylinder units, and have the advantage of fewer working parts. If they were less smooth than sixes, this was of little concern, as traditional vehicles with draughty driving compartments and hard tyres were not renowned for comfort.

However, all this changed with the demand for extra power to take full advantage of the maximum speed limit for pneumatic tyred heavy lorries which had been raised to 20 mph in 1928. Incidentally, many converted lorries were given only pneumatic front tyres in the mistaken belief that this qualified them for extra speed, while leaving the actual load-carrying to tyres that could not blow-out.

The first ordinary six cylinder heavy commercial vehicles had been produced by Halley in 1919, but these had not sold successfully, probably as much due to the difficult economic climate as to any in-built operator resistance, though the petrol companies bought a few 3 to 4 tonners, probably confirming operators' worst fears about fuel consumption. The chief impact of the six cylinder Halley chassis was in the passenger field, notably for 25-35 seat charabancs and coaches, and for fire engines.

Sixes came to the fore in 1927, with offerings from Guy, Karrier, Maudslay, Thornycroft and others, but again they were for passenger service, and it was not until 1929 that they seriously began to be employed for goods haulage. Another case where the six did well was the limousine-style American light trucks which became so popular in Britain from the mid Twenties, largely thanks to competitive pricing. Several firms supplied them, notably Chevrolet, Reo, International and Graham/Dodge. They were primarily in the 30 cwt to 2½ ton class, but their excellent combination of performance, light weight and comfort endeared

them to drivers, and the new generation of models in the Thirties gradually moved into the lower end of the heavy class. This caused the traditional, low volume, high quality heavy truck makers to retreat into the heavier field, out of the increasingly competitive 3-5 ton market.

This growing competitiveness was sparked off by General Motors' decision to produce an anglicised version of their successful Chevrolet truck in Britain, using largely British-made parts. The resulting Bedford began in 1931 as a six cylinder 2 tonner, but quickly moved into the medium category when operators discovered that its lack of traditional engineering refinement, and correspondingly shorter life with intensive use, was often more than offset by its low price. It did not take a mathematical genius to see that a 100,000 mile expectancy from a chassis costing say £300 was at least as good as a better vehicle capable of quarter of a million miles, but costing more than twice as much.

Ford's Dagenham plant opened at about the same time, and was soon producing comparable vehicles; meanwhile Dodge did the same at Kew, and Reo imported American parts and aimed further upmarket. All these vehicles, especially when given extra payload potential with trailing third axles or articulated trailers, were more than adequate for own-account operators (manufacturers transporting their own goods) doing local delivery, low mileage work, or for owner/driver or tipper operators, who could expect only a short and arduous life for their vehicles, regardless of first cost. There was of course still an important demand for the handbuilt expensive chassis for haulage work above about 5 tons when they were expected to work fully laden for most of the time, but the cheaper medium chassis played an important and growing role throughout the Thirties, largely due to legislation which took effect from the beginning of 1934. This was based on the Salter Report of 1932, which decided to base the

9

incidence of road costs on the 23.5 million ton miles travelled annually by commercial vehicles, and to recover this cost in fuel tax and licence duty levied according to unladen weight. Because of the disproportionately high road damage caused by high individual axle weights, the smaller types of goods vehicle were encouraged by lower road tax. Thus 2 to 3 tons unladen weight, corresponding to ·the typical 4/5 tonner, paid £30 on pneumatics and £40 on solids, and 5/6 tons unladen weight paid £90 duty, or £120 for solid tyres. This gave additional impetus to medium vehicles, and it encouraged some operators to run two cheap 3 ton mass-produced vehicles rather than one heavy expensive vehicle. Heavy makers like Thornycroft felt that this made a mockery of the law as it encouraged overloading of vehicles with insufficient inbuilt strength to cope with it, and at the same time put more vehicles than necessary on the road. Their grievances were further aggravated by a special concession for vehicles under 2½ tons unladen, which not only paid less duty but were also permitted to travel at 30 mph.

Thus, there was a real incentive for the mass-producers to make lightweight medium vehicles, and the field was soon split between the American backed manufacturers and the two principal British makers of cheap vehicles, Morris-Commercial and Commer. The former had specialised in light vehicles, apart from a brief and unsuccessful attempt from 1929 in the heavy market. Commer, since its takeover by Rootes in 1928, had been gradually moving away from its traditional heavy market to the mass-sales area where Rootes were able to obtain production economies by using certain parts from their larger cars.

These makers designed vehicles able to carry the maximum possible payload under the 2½ tons unladen limit. They were joined in the later Thirties by some of the traditional makers like Dennis and Leyland, offering very scientifically engineered models such as the Light 5-Tonner and the Lynx, which provided previously unequalled cost/ton/miles productivity figures. The £30 and 30 mph class also bred some new manufacturers like Jensen and Seddon, and led to detailed research by manufacturers into lightweight materials and scientifically stressed parts which were no heavier than strictly necessary to do the job for which they were intended. This reduction in metal helped to keep prices down and was an important contributory factor to British lorries being the most widely exported in the world.

Meanwhile it was not only in design that road haulage was becoming more complex. New legislation was introduced at the time of the new road duty which differentiated for the first time between the various classes of lorry user. Own-account operators required C licences; haulage contractors more expensive A licences; and businesses carrying their own goods, and also others for reward, B licences. Along with these licences came stricter employment regulations to limit drivers' hours, and operators had to be able to satisfy licencing authorities of their ability to maintain their vehicles safely, and to be providing a service not already obtainable from someone else. Though widely mistrusted, and expected to give the railways an unfair advantage, these regulations did much to make road haulage less cut-throat, and in the long term more profitable and efficient − a factor in its continued success and growth, and, ironically, of its gradual supremacy over the railways.

Meanwhile, to return to vehicle design, perhaps the most significant development of the entire period, in fact of heavy road haulage in its entire history, was the arrival of the diesel engine.

Diesel, or heavy oil, or compression ignition, as the engines were variously called, had first appeared in a few goods vehicles on the continent in 1923, but it was not until the late Twenties that the principal protagonists MAN, Benz, and Saurer successfully began to exploit the tremendous advantage in fuel cost and consumption that their engines provided. MAN vehicles were not sold in Britain, but from 1927 Mercedes-Benz and, from 1928, Saurer diesel lorries became available, and soon made a tremendous impact, if not on operators, at least on other British manufacturers.

The attraction of the oil engine was that it was able to run on the cruder oils from lower down the fractionating process used to obtain petrol. It originally cost only about 4 old pence per gallon until duty was levied, and even then was far cheaper than petrol. The diesel engine could also cover twice as many miles per gallon as an equivalent petrol-engined vehicle.

All the major heavy vehicle makers who already produced their own petrol engines, as opposed to buying them from specialist suppliers like Dorman, quickly started development work on their own diesels. AEC, in 1928, was the first British maker to have its own unit running, and Garrett was not far behind, this time using a proprietary McLaren engine made under licence in Britain from Benz. The AEC engine took some three years to perfect, by which time AEC had won its independence from the London Underground Group, and had become a major goods vehicle, as well as bus, supplier. Another important innovation was the experimental use of the Gardner marine engine in a number of makes of buses and converted petrol-engined lorries. Then in 1930, Pagefield became the first British maker to introduce a new chassis design especially intended for the diesel engine.

The Gardner L2 engine was astonishingly successful because it was beautifully made and had no bearing troubles like the units evolved from lower compression petrol engines. It was very efficient and therefore extremely economical. In 1931 it was joined by the LW version, which was designed from the outset to be as light as possible for use in commercial vehicles. Not only was it highly economical but also very reliable, and capable of at least a quarter of a million miles without extensive overhaul.

It was this engine which helped Foden to make the smooth transition from steam in 1931, and it was also available in six other important makes of chassis that year, and before long in many more, including Maudslay and Scammell. Leyland followed soon afterwards with their own successful engine, and by 1935 Dennis, Thornycroft, Crossley and Albion had appeared with their own units.

Some other makes of engine were also satisfactory, including Blackstone, originally used by Atkinson, and Dorman-Ricardo, used by Yorkshire and others. Most of the Dorman units were comparatively small and suited vehicles of around 3 to 4 tons capacity. Another make to appear for lighter vehicles was the Perkins. In its own way, this became almost as important as the Gardner because it enabled vehicles from 2 tons capacity upwards to gain the benefits of diesel power. Its quantity production soon brought its price down to within reach of a similar petrol engine, whilst its light weight made it suitable for the new breed of light weight vehicles like the 6 ton Seddon in 1938.

One other important diesel stepping stone in the 1930s was the Armstrong-Saurer. This was the Swiss Saurer produced in Britain by the major engineering firm of Sir W. G. Armstrong Whitworth, and it had a highly successful run between 1931 and 1937 in maximum capacity four, six and eight wheel models. The patents covering its engine design were then adopted by Morris-Commercial, who became the first mass-produced chassis makers to provide their own diesels, though the war interrupted development before they could become generally available.

Mention of rigid eight wheelers marks another

early Thirties development pioneered by Sentinel Steam Waggons in 1930. AEC, Armstrong-Saurer, ERF and Leyland all offered this new class of diesel-engined 14 to 15 ton capacity vehicle by the end of 1934, and other heavy makers like Foden and Albion followed soon afterwards. Yet another new configuration to appear was the twin-steer six wheeler introduced by ERF in 1937 and adopted by Foden, Leyland, Dennis and others. This had a single driven back axle with the two front steering axles as on a rigid eight. It gave a similar payload on trunk routes to a conventional rigid six but saved a little unladen weight and reduced tyre scrub.

It is interesting to note that the relative numbers of heavy vehicles were declining steadily in the Thirties when compared with the under 2½ ton unladen category which had increased in importance by about 6 per cent between 1930 and 1935. Though relatively small in numbers, heavy vehicles were responsible for the bulk of the nation's long distance transport and as size increased fewer large vehicles were needed to carry ever increasing payloads. During the same period there was a dramatic growth in the number of articulated vehicles – many of them fairly light rigid vehicles converted to carry double the payload using a superimposed trailer. According to the Ministry of Transport Census 1935, 818 vehicles on the road in 1930 were articulated and 7,021 were licensed for towing drawbar trailers. By 1935 the articulated figure had increased to 4,792 and the trailer towers had fallen to 5,729.

By the late Thirties, heavy vehicle design and operating requirements had changed out of all comparison with those of only twenty years earlier. Vehicles had shed weight and yet gone up in capacity; they could travel at double the speed of their predecessors but stop in a shorter distance; they were safer and far more comfortable, and all their technical innovations of the past decade were about to be tested in the most mechanised war to date. From about 1937, several manufacturers like Morris, Guy, Garner and Thornycroft began to concentrate increasingly on military lorries, and several of the others added military models to their ranges.

One overriding preoccupation was that when the inevitable war took place, Britain would be cut off from supplies of petroleum products, and the country's road haulage would grind to a halt. Various alternative fuel sources were considered, with steam produced from British coal a strong contender. However, even Sentinel could see that the inevitably higher unladen weight of the steam lorry, and the gradual disappearance of drivers who understood its intricacies, spelt the need for something more simple. They, along with many others, explored the prospects of running vehicles on gas produced in plants actually carried on the vehicle. They were quite successful, as had been Guy and Thornycroft before them, but in fact petrol supplies were maintained, and the diesel was left to reign supreme at the heavy end of the nation's goods transport.

The typical lorry had come a very long way in only twenty short years.

The enormous growth in heavy road haulage during the Twenties was considerably influenced by the flood of cheap ex-WD vehicles that came on the market and by the enormous numbers of servicemen taught to drive during the war. Here Bill Bouts, who with his brother was to run one of the biggest fleets of all, stands beside one of the ruggedest of all the 1914/18 lorries, the 32 hp Albion. Though driven by chain, and rather underpowered even by the standards of the time, these 3 tonners worked for many years in the Twenties carrying far heavier loads than ever originally intended.

Typical of the thousands of American ex-service vehicles which entered civilian haulage in Britain after World War I, often at rock-bottom prices. This is a Selden, but there were at least ten other popular makes in the 3 to 4 ton class. Most heavy American vehicles of the time had chain drive, and wooden spoked wheels were commonplace. Vehicles of this sort were the first vehicles in numerous haulage fleets that were built up from nothing in the Twenties.

Many post-war vehicles were identical in design to their ex-WD counterparts so it is often difficult to tell them apart if the ex-WD vehicles have been rebodied. This tank is mounted on an AEC Y type 3 ton chassis of which no less than 10,000 were produced during the war, making AEC the largest British supplier of Subsidy lorries. They were able to mass-produce lorries because of their pre-war experience with supplying London's buses, and because they installed one of the first moving production lines in Europe. AEC and Daimler were closely linked at the time and produced similar vehicles.

The Hallford was a well-known pioneer make originally based on the Swiss Saurer and made at Dartford in Kent by a firm now best known for its refrigeration equipment and lifts. Like many other heavy lorry makers Hallford was badly affected by the slump after World War I and abandoned manufacture in the mid Twenties. This is an early post-war example and shows a typically Hallford feature of a radiator built horizontally, so that its side, and not its top and bottom, tanks were detachable and carried the cooling tubes.

Steam played an important part in extra-heavy transport during the Twenties and to a lesser extent in the Thirties. This mid Twenties Atkinson was used as a tractor for hauling drawbar trailers and was still in use around Liverpool's dockland as late as 1953. Atkinson successfully made the change to diesel power in the early Thirties after a difficult time during the Depression when their steam waggons would not sell and they were forced to diversify into trailers and four to six wheel chassis conversions.

The famous 32 hp wartime Albion seen here in civilian guise. The canvas screen was all that protected the driver from the elements.

Above Early Twenties steam waggons normally had horizontal boilers running fore and aft like the Foden, or vertically like the Sentinel. This Yorkshire was an eccentric but successful design in which the boiler ran across the frame. Tanks as opposed to individual cans first came into common use for transporting liquid fuels in the Twenties. This particular combination was not as lethal as it might appear since steam vehicles were permitted to carry fuel oil (which was not highly inflammable) but not petrol.

Right Another view of the unusual Yorkshire design. Note the flap at the bottom for releasing ash and clinker and the typical oil sidelights of the period.

17

Left Thornycroft had supplied around 5,000 J type models to the Services in World War I. This example is probably not war-surplus but a new version of the famous model built in 1922, either a J or its very similar Q or W sisters, which could carry up to 5 and 6 tons respectively, instead of the 3½ to 4 tons of the uprated J. All had the same T-head 40 hp engine until 1924, when their valves were moved to one side to make an L-head.

Below Pagefield built around 500 Subsidy vehicles during the war and this 1923 F model 3½ tonner is closely related to them. It has a Dorman 40 hp petrol engine, a separately mounted four speed gearbox and, unusually for the time, a rear axle located by radius rods to keep it from reacting to the twisting effect of shaft drive. Electric lighting was a safety feature with petrol tankers some time before it became general practice on normal goods models.

Perhaps the most famous of all the ex-WD vehicles was the R.A.F.-type Leyland, of which some 3,000 were reconditioned during the Twenties at Leyland's Kingston factory outside London. This factory was later to be where the Leyland Cub was produced, and had originated during the war as an armaments works. Many R.A.F.-types were in general use for over twenty years and at the end were hardly recognisable with their modified enclosed cabs and pneumatic tyres. Note the rack on this example for carrying empty biscuit tins.

Leyland are not normally associated with steam vehicles because from 1904 their principal efforts were put into the development of the petrol engine. However, right up until 1926 they could supply steam lorries, and this example made in 1919 was sent to Australia. Following the end of Leyland steam lorry production their spares and service were taken over by Atkinson, who also bought the remnants of Mann´s steam parts.

This 1919 Halley 3 tonner made near the Albion factory in Glasgow by Scotland´s second largest heavy lorry maker was very unusual in having six cylinders. Apart from special purpose vehicles, like fire engines, four cylinders were standard practice in other heavy vehicles until the late Twenties. The six cylinder 35 hp Halley was not a significant sales success, though it became quite popular as the basis for smooth, refined passenger coaches and charabancs, as well as fire engines which were a Halley speciality.

Like Hallford, Straker-Squire was a firm which did well before and during World War I but never really recovered from the slump in sales that followed.

Here is a typical line-up of immediately post-war 3 to 5 ton models which were soon replaced by a very advanced A model. Operators were sceptical about the A's unusual slipper spring pads on the suspension, its propshaft unsupported by a centre bearing, and its two ball-bearing crankshaft, and these eccentricities contributed to Straker-Squire's downfall during the mid Twenties.

One of the most unusual vehicles to achieve success in the Twenties was the Tilling-Stevens. Although some had conventional gearboxes the firm's real claim to fame was its petrol-electric transmission. In this the engine worked a generator which in turn powered an electric motor which drove the back axle via a conventional propshaft. The driver only had to move a lever to select the required speed. The system was particularly popular on buses, where it left the driver free to concentrate on his passengers and urban traffic. It had the drawback of rather leisurely performance.

Right A steamer in its element. This 1923 Foden weighs a colossal 6½ tons unladen and yet has a nominal payload of 5½ tons. However this is just the sort of application where the steamer excelled as its weight is of secondary importance in specialised work like road building. This example is carrying macadam plant, and the coal for its burner of course presents no problem. Note the coiled hose for collecting water for the waggon's boiler from ponds, streams, or special hydrants.

MEX FUEL OIL

SHELL MEX LTD. KINGSWAY.

Far left Articulation was an obvious way of increasing the payload capacity of a rigid chassis. Scammell were unusual in actually producing complete articulated outfits for many years before they even made their first rigid. This is a very early 1921 or 1922 example able to carry 10 tons and equipped with a 45 hp engine, a three forward speed gearbox and chain drive. Before long Scammell adopted cylindrical tanks with pumps driven off the front of the crankshaft for loading and unloading. The Scammell Six Wheeler did much to extend the popularity of petrol engined vehicles into the realm of the steamer.

Despite its hefty build this 1920 Guy was only rated as a 2½ tonner. However, nearly all quality vehicles of the time were able to carry at least a 50 per cent overload, a fact reluctantly endorsed by many of the manufacturers, and soon afterwards Guy hinted that this 25 hp machine was capable of more when they reclassified it as a 2½/3 tonner. Until 1928 this was Guy's heaviest goods model, though from the mid Twenties they made far larger passenger chassis, some with three axles.

This 2-type AEC was the first of its make to join the fleet of Shell-Mex in 1925. The petrol companies were amongst the most important users of heavy vehicles in the Twenties, their resources naturally being behind internal combustion engined road vehicles rather than the steam driven railways. By now cabs had acquired doors and windscreens, though the driver was still not totally protected from the weather.

One of the best imported chassis of the mid Twenties was the Saurer from Switzerland. It was of high quality and very expensive and featured a number of interesting refinements. These included a starting handle which automatically retarded the ignition timing to avoid backfiring when turned, a special camshaft to increase the effect of engine braking, and the built-in tool tray shown. In 1925 the 5/6 ton model became the first of its size to feature pneumatic tyres. Saurer introduced their diesel model to Britain in 1928 and from 1931 this was made under licence in Newcastle-on-Tyne as the Armstrong-Saurer.

A 4 ton Karrier of the mid Twenties. The makers had previously
used Dorman and Tylor engines for this weight range but had
recently developed their own 40 hp four cylinder unit. Karrier
was an important manufacturer in the Twenties, but they ran
into difficulties during the Great Slump as they offered too many
models, each with limited sales appeal. They also wasted
money on the development of three axle passenger vehicles.
However, their experience with municipal vehicles and
mechanical horses saved them for long enough to be bought by
Rootes in 1934 and associated with Commer.

Above An impressive 1926 7 ton Maudslay. Maudslays were unusual in a number of ways — they had always favoured overhead valve engines, normally associated with high performance cars of the time. They were also amongst the earliest users of forward control on heavy vehicles and offered one of the highest four wheel model payload capacities of the time — with suitable lightweight bodywork 8 tons was possible on the 36/70 hp model shown. Through most of the Twenties and Thirties Maudslay output was small; in their best year 1919 they sold 348 vehicles.

Far right Another early articulated vehicle, this time a mid Twenties Halley, which was used as a street sprinkler by the City of Birmingham Public Works Department. Though by now chain drive had all but disappeared on lighter vehicles it was still popular for the heaviest lorries or where there was the likelihood of axle breakages, as with on-off road tippers. Two-wheel brakes remained common on heavy four wheel chassis right up to 1930.

Right It is impossible to date this Leyland exactly without its registration number. It is on pneumatics, yet restricted to 12 mph. Therefore, it was built before the limit was increased to 20 mph in 1928. Pneumatic tyres were only just becoming available for lorries around the 30 cwt level in 1923 and as this is on twin tyres it is obviously a lot heavier, probably the 3 ton 32 hp C model. The acetylene head and oil side lamps suggest early Twenties, so 1925 will not be far from correct.

The Bristol Tramways and Carriage Company was
primarily a bus operator which had started its
own chassis department before World War I to
supply its own buses. Before long Bristol was
supplying other operators with both buses and
lorries. However its goods vehicle output was
never large and indeed was almost entirely
stopped in the Thirties. This is a rare 1925 4 ton
Bristol with a four cylinder 40 hp engine. It is seen
carrying a 1,200 gallon three compartment spirit
tank.

Ultra-heavy haulage was the province of steam in the Twenties and to a lesser extent in the Thirties. Traction engines did the really big jobs whilst more agile steam tractors like this Foden could cope with over 30 tons gross train weight when used to pull a road train. This example was used by an amusement caterer for towing his fairground rides and incorporated a big generator on the hornplate above the boiler for power and illumination on site.

For a little over a year the Associated Equipment Company (AEC) and Daimler Company amalgamated their sales and technical expertise and their products were jointly sold as Associated Daimler (ADC). They could have AEC four cylinder poppet valve or Daimler six cylinder sleeve valve engines, the latter normally used in Daimler luxury cars. This ADC is a 4/5 ton model of 1927 and soon afterwards the two firms went their separate ways, AEC to make both trucks and buses, whilst Daimler concentrated on passenger vehicles.

Left The rigid six wheeler first appeared in Britain in 1924, but took some time to become popular for heavy goods haulage as it suffered from excessive tyre wear, particularly when the vehicle was fitted with solids. It was not until the late Twenties, when giant pneumatics were commonplace, that the layout became really successful. This 10 ton capacity Leyland SWQ2 was built in 1928 and used single tyres on its middle axle to minimise tyre scrub.

Below The advanced Super Sentinel range of undertype steam waggons appeared in 1923 as nominal 6 ton four wheelers or 12 ton artics. They were further refined in 1927 as the DG range and now included the DG6 rigid six wheeler shown here on the Holyhead road near Shrewsbury. It could carry a load of between 10 and 15 tons and had a two cylinder poppet valve steam engine, two forward gears (adequate because of its near-constant torque) with built-in differential and chain drive to one rear axle, which then drove the other by further chains.

Far left Most rigid six wheelers in the mid Twenties were lightweight models given an extra axle solely to improve their off-road traction and floatation and usually built to military specification. When Scammell produced their first rigid vehicle in 1927 it was a heavy 6 tonner made with colonial, as well as military, orders in mind. Initially with 6 x 4 drive, it was available from 1929 as the all-wheel-drive Pioneer. The 6 x 4 example shown has temporary tracks on the rear wheels to improve traction.

Having got into considerable financial difficulties in 1922, Commer had a very tough period until they were saved from oblivion in 1926 by Humber, who were in turn bought two years later by the Rootes brothers. This 1,000 gallon tanker is built on the chassis that finally replaced the old chain drive RC model in 1928. With changing regulations to encourage the use of pneumatic tyres that year, it was one of the last vehicles on solids to be bought by Shell-Mex.

1000 GALLON ROAD WAGON TANK (REGISTERED DESIGN)
MANUFACTURED BY
THE STEEL BARREL CO. LD. UXBRIDGE.

Another cross-country six wheeler first introduced in 1927 was the FWD 6 tonner. Unlike the Scammell it had 6 x 6 drive from the outset, because it was based on the British version of the famous American Four Wheel Drive lorry which always had a driven front axle. In common with many expensive, special-purpose vehicles this example had a very long life, ending its days in the 1960s with an amusement caterer, who found its inbuilt winch invaluable. From 1929 British FWD was associated with AEC and used many common parts.

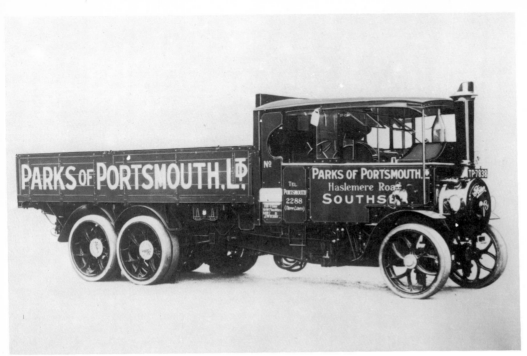

Both Sentinel and, in this case, Foden were early converts to rigid six wheelers as steamers were at their most economical when worked intensively at full load. This 10 to 12 tonner was built in about 1929 and marked the zenith of Foden's traditional design of steam waggon. Because of their ability to handle concentrated heavy loads economically, steamers were always popular with brewers, flour millers and quarry owners. However, the taxation based on unladen weight introduced in 1933 quickly decimated their numbers.

Though always rugged and reliable with no unnecessary frills Albion vehicles nearly always looked more old-fashioned than they actually were. In an attempt to change their image, in 1927 they introduced this very modernistic 4 tonner which had a faired-in radiator and attractive bow front. In fact the only things to suggest that it was not made ten years later are the open cab sides. Like many designs ahead of their time it was not a sales success and Albion soon reverted to their traditional radiator design, which was still current over twenty years later.

Left The Garner lorry was popular for medium loads in the Twenties and Thirties. Initially made in the United States for Henry Garner, a Birmingham motor dealer, they were produced in Britain using local parts from 1925. This 65 cwt model of 1929 used a Dorman 25 hp engine and is seen here in the livery of Russian Oil Products. Most contemporary Garners had forward control though, as in this case, normal control was available for operators who did not require long load platforms and preferred extra engine accessibility.

Below The traditional Scammell design of articulated vehicle had changed very little by 1929. It was suitable for 12 to 20 ton loads and it still featured the original design of four cylinder engine and chain drive. This example is of note for its two pairs of two short trailer axles mounted side by side, and its frameless tank, which was designed to be self-supporting without the need for a sub-frame. The driver was particularly exposed though he had canvas and perspex sidescreens for the worst weather.

Heavy rigid six wheelers really started to become popular with the arrival of suitable pneumatic tyres following the 1928 legislation. This allowed pneumatic tyred heavy vehicles to pay less road tax and to travel at 20 mph instead of 12 mph. On rigid sixes it also gave the advantage of considerably reduced tyre wear. The example illustrated is a 7/8 ton Karrier KW6 operated by British Petroleum, who found that the extra chassis length of a medium six wheeler helped them to reduce tank diameter and therefore centre of gravity.

Above In 1929 Dennis offered 6 ton six wheel versions of their very popular 4 ton model. Dennis were one of the largest commercial vehicle makers of the time who in 1927 had considered taking over Guy, and in 1929 had even had merger talks with Leyland. Their output was less than AEC and Leyland, but on a par with Thornycroft. Their engines were produced in Coventry by the once famous firm of White and Poppe, whom Dennis had taken over in 1918 and whose facilities were finally moved to the Dennis factory at Guildford in 1932.

Left Another firm to make a special effort in the heavy goods six wheeler market was Thornycroft, who had been producing light examples for military requirements since the mid Twenties. This is a 10 ton JC tipper used by the London Midland and Scottish Railway on track laying and maintenance work, and was first introduced late in 1929. By then hydraulics were sufficiently advanced to be suitable for tipping bodies to replace the clumsy rope or worm mechanical systems, or the hand screws previously fitted to lighter vehicles.

The Scammell rigid four wheeler appeared in 1929 as a nominal 6 tonner. It still featured the old four cylinder engine, now developing 80 hp, but could now have a Kirkstall worm drive live back axle as an option to the chain drive shown here. The six wheel rigid Scammell described on page 30 also had shaft drive, though it had a different final drive arrangement in which the rear wheels on each side were mounted at the outer ends of gear cases which pivoted round a single driving axle. This gave maximum wheel articulation when working off the road and a higher overall gear reduction.

The Reo was one of the most successful medium trucks available from America. It was sold by Harris and Hasell of London and Bristol during the Twenties. Reo then established their own sales network which led Harris and Hasell to develop their own BAT 2 ton or twenty seat chassis. This was only available briefly in 1929/30. Meanwhile Reo continued to do well with their Speed Wagons, so named on account of their comparatively high power, usually six cylinder engines. Their performance was liked by coach operators and for livestock transport.

Left Though by no stretch of the imagination a heavy vehicle, the Shelvoke and Drewry chassis for local deliveries was in fact rated as a 2½ tonner in its lightest form and up to a 4 tonner in its heaviest. Its small wheels made loading and unloading easy. It had tiller steering and, as in the case of this 1928/9 example, a 15.9 hp petrol engine mounted transversely in the box alongside the driver. S & D vehicles were, and still are, primarily popular for such municipal duties as refuse collection. Similar vehicles were briefly made by Easyloader, Garner and Vulcan.

Far left A light six wheeler by Thornycroft on single tyres. This is a 1929 XB 5 ton model where length more than carrying capacity was important to reduce tank height. Petroleum regulations required the fire screen of steel and asbestos that can be seen fitted behind the cab. It extended under the frame to isolate the exhaust system from the inflammable load. Note the bulb horn, that typical feature of vintage days, sticking through the bulkhead.

Above In 1930 Pagefield were producing conventional goods models as well as the lorry-mounted-crane and refuse collection vehicles illustrated.

The crane was designed for handling containers from railway waggons to lorries and vice versa. The Pagefield System was an ingenious design evolved in 1922 in which horses towed refuse containers from house to house whilst the lorry shuttled loaded containers to the nearest dump. These containers were winched on and off the lorry, enabling it to keep pace with four or five collection teams.

The AEC Majestic first appeared at the end of 1929. It was a 6 tonner and had a six cylinder 45 hp petrol engine developing 110 bhp, and was similar to the ones used in the contemporary Regal and Regent passenger models. It was one of a whole range of new AEC goods models bearing such famous names as Mammoth, Mercury and Monarch. It marked a new and concerted attack by AEC on the heavy goods market – traditionally dominated by such firms as Leyland and Dennis – which AEC had been neglecting whilst producing London buses.

The heaviest version of the Ford Model A produced in England in the late Twenties was the AAF for 30 cwts. However when converted to a six wheeler this capacity was comfortably doubled. Several firms undertook these conversions, of which the best known were by County Commercial Cars Ltd of Fleet, Hampshire. Those with single drive were given the model name Surrey whilst 6 x 4s were called Sussex. Similar conversions were made to several light mass-produced chassis of the time to increase their payload.

In the Twenties Vulcan particularly specialised in low-load chassis, which were popular with municipalities. The example shown is a 3XL 3 ton capacity model of 1929 with dustless refuse collection bodywork. So many lorry manufacturers were forced to specialise in municipal vehicles, by the fall in demand of their general models in the Slump, that this too became highly competitive.

After their remarkable success in the 20-30 cwt market Morris-Commercial started in 1929 to build heavier four wheelers at the newly acquired Wolseley works. The first of these was the 3 ton capacity Leader available with forward or normal control. Despite being the lowest priced vehicle of its carrying capacity in 1931, it never achieved much sales success, because of the Slump, and only about 1,300 were sold in its four year existence. Still heavier Morris models fared even worse until the introduction of the C range in 1933.

At various times passenger chassis have been used for special goods purposes, notably maximum capacity pantechnicons. That this 1930 AEC chassis was designed as a bus is shown by the drop frame with swept-up sections over the axles. It was chosen for this application to keep the centre of gravity of the petrol tank as low as possible. AECs were popular for this purpose but other makes were also used, including drop frame six wheelers.

The Garrett QL 10/15 ton six wheel steam lorry was rather more expensive than the contemporary Sentinel and generally considered to be not as good. Only a few more than 100 were produced from its introduction in 1928 to the end of the company in 1931. In 1932 Garrett were bought by the famous railway locomotive manufacturers, Beyer, Peacock & Co. Ltd, and thereafter they abandoned steam waggons though built a few electric vehicles and experimental diesel lorries.

Steam still continued to be popular for heavy haulage, especially in timber extraction where most of the work tended to be fairly local. One of the chief drawbacks to steam vehicles was their limited range between water stops. In summer steamers would soon pump brooks near main roads dry and it was not every road authority that was willing to install special hydrants. Fodens, like this 1929 example, were popular for timber work and after steam vehicle production ended Foden continued to make diesel timber tractors. Some of these used up old steam chassis parts and bore a close resemblance to steam vehicles.

Guy were enthusiastic advocates of the rigid six wheel layout, yet strangely were never very successful in the 10-12 ton class, which became popular in 1929/30. The vehicle shown is a far lighter type, for 3-5 tons, and is based on the popular Subsidy-type six wheeler which Guy had been producing in quantity since 1926. Subsidy chassis differed from commercial models chiefly because of their rear suspension design which pivoted from a central trunnion and which allowed considerable wheel articulation in rough off-road service.

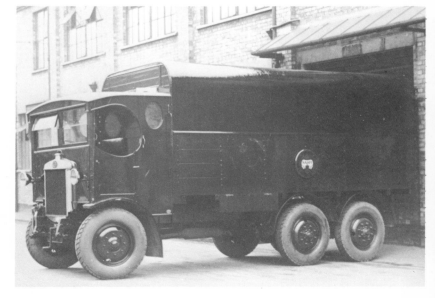

The Monarch was the 4 ton model in the new range announced
by AEC in 1929/30. Unlike the Majestic shown on page 40, it
used a four cylinder engine shared with the 3½ ton Mercury. This
example dates from 1930 and is interesting for the oil side
lamps still fitted, though they appear to be optionally wired for
electricity. Electric lighting had become standard practice by
then, but on some vehicles, particularly ones with self starters, it
paid to keep the battery in peak condition and use oil lamps
when parking for any length of time.

At the same time that AEC introduced their new range of goods
models each beginning with the letter M, Leyland introduced
their directly competitive T range at the 1929 Commercial Motor
Show. These had many of the animal names that were to
become a famous Leyland feature in the Thirties. Shown here is
a 1930 four cylinder Bison 4½/5½ tonner. Though heavy
vehicles of the period had prominent starting handles, these
were usually only for use as a last resort if the recently
arrived electric self starter failed to function.

WORLD'S BIGGEST TRANSPORT FEAT, 170 Tons BY ROAD.

WORLDS LARGEST TRANSFORMER 125,000 MA HACK WA

M·R·S LIMITED

KD·9168

HEAVY TRANSPORT

For many years after its introduction in 1929 the Scammell 100 tonner was the biggest lorry in the world. A small number were built and this is one being used for the sort of ultra heavy haulage feat previously reserved for teams of traction engines. Though soon converted to diesel these tractors started life with the 80 bhp four cylinder petrol engine from their far smaller sisters, and did one mile per gallon. Drive was taken by chain to the tractor's back axle; this was divided in the middle and shod with 8 solid rubber tyres.

An example of AEC´s heaviest four wheel model in 1930, the aptly named Mammoth 7-8 tonner, which was mechanically similar to the normal control Majestic. It was also available from 1931 in rigid six wheel form as the Mammoth Major and could then carry 12 tons. In 1934 the Mammoths were joined by a rigid eight wheel sister called the Mammoth Major 8 for 15 ton loads. Note the legal requirement to carry notice of its speed limit on the side of the chassis – 20 mph because it is on pneumatics, but reduced to 12 mph when towing a trailer.

A 12 ton capacity Thornycroft QC six wheeler supplied in 1931 for delivering 2,300 gallons of milk from West Country creameries to London. It has a 103 bhp six cylinder petrol engine and typifies the heavy long distance trunk vehicle of the time. Lorry-mounted refrigeration plants were not in general use for another thirty years so the milk was kept cold by extensive insulation and aluminium cladding. Thornycroft were a major name in heavy trucking throughout the Thirties, though overseas and military vehicles occupied much of their Basingstoke works.

Above Dennis had first introduced their 10-12 ton six wheeler in 1929 as the model M. However, this was basically for a bus that had not gone into production and it was soon replaced by this more robust straight-framed model. The example shown was built in 1931 for carrying 2,500 gallons of petrol in a five-compartment tank. Note the servo unit on the side of the chassis, a development which gave mechanical assistance to the driver's braking effort.

Left The British diesel engine came to road haulage in 1930. Prior to that a few foreign diesels, notably Saurer and Mercedes-Benz, had been running, but in 1930 a number of old chassis were converted with the new Gardner L2 range of marine engines. Amongst the first was this R.A.F.-type Leyland. The Gardner L2 engine had been offered since 1929 for marine use, but it was first in service in a bus in March 1930, some time before it took to the water.

The first vehicle actually to be fitted from new with a Gardner engine was this Pagefield in September 1930. It is shown here on test before entering service in Burton-on-Trent. It covered 115,000 troublefree miles over the next 2½ years, at around 16 mpg, and 10 mpg when used with a trailer at an all-up weight of 15¼ tons. In all some 200 Gardner L2 engines were installed in commercial vehicle chassis before a new LW (lightweight) range specifically designed for road work was introduced in 1931.

Tilling-Stevens, or TSM as they had temporarily been renamed after financial difficulties, offered Gardner LW engines in their range from 1931. This rigid six wheeler, however, is a conversion carried out by the manufacturer and Chivers in order to try a five cylinder 5L2 engine. Tilling-Stevens never became important for goods vehicles in the Thirties, though their passenger chassis, now with gear as opposed to petrol-electric-drive, sold well.

Foden bowed to the inevitable in 1931 and began to build diesel lorries powered by the new LW Gardner diesel engines. This is the first made, which, years later, the manufacturers bought back and still own. It has over a million miles to its credit. For a time Foden also offered petrol engines by Austin and Meadows in their lightest models but these were not a sales success and thereafter Foden stuck to the medium and heavy market and exclusively to the diesel engine.

Numerous firms started to build diesel engines for commercial vehicle use though Gardner, Dorman and Perkins were the most successful of the outside suppliers. Most major lorry makers who produced their own petrol engines soon developed their own diesels.

A small firm to rely on outside suppliers was Shefflex who used the unusual Petter three cylinder two-stroke diesel from 1932. Early Shefflex lorries carried under 3 tons, though from 1930 the firm supplied the majority with extra axles to provide a 5 ton payload.

Garner continued to specialise in medium capacity models in the Thirties and even this apparently hefty six wheeler of 1932 was only rated for a nominal 4 ton 4 cwt payload. They had close ties with Sentinel, who wanted to be ready to move into the petrol and diesel field quickly if steam waggons were further penalised by law.

This TW60 model had hinge-out wings and lower cab sides to allow a fitter to stand next to the chassis and do maintenance or repair work to the engine.

Right It was unusual for rigid goods models to retain the bonneted layout of this Leyland Bison in the Thirties. Operators were anxious to have the greatest possible load space and normally opted for forward control. However, this 1932 Leyland is carrying a dense 1,200 gallon load of petrol so additional space is unnecessary. To reduce unladen taxable weight to the minimum, aluminium has been used for the cab and other parts, thereby saving 6 cwt.

Below A new make of vehicle that was to become important in the heavy field appeared in 1933. Shown is the first ERF to be built, and it was developed by Edwin Foden who had formerly worked for the family firm of Fodens. The first few were built in sheds in and around Sandbach before a proper factory was acquired. They were powered by the new Gardner LW diesel engines. ERF soon followed with multiwheelers, including the first twin-steer six wheeler in 1937.

Though a number of the more important manufacturers had their own body departments where cabs and bodywork could be fitted to customer requirements, the majority of vehicles were supplied as bare chassis or chassis/cabs to be fitted with bodies by specialists. Here a consignment of Fords await conversion into vans. The third chassis from the front on the left is one of the new Bedfords, introduced by General Motors in 1931. These chassis are all officially designated 2 tonners though in practice they will undoubtedly often carry more.

Above Both Scammell and Karrier became important
makers of 3 and 6 ton capacity mechanical horses. Karrier
were first in 1931 followed by Scammell in 1933 with this
early production 3 ton model. Scammell eventually built
over 20,000 tractors and 100,000 trailers which, as well as
demonstrating the success of the idea, illustrates how
one tractor could work with many trailers. The secret was
a quickly detachable coupling which allowed the tractor
to deliver one loaded trailer whilst another was left at base
for loading.

Below A handsome AEC tanker of 1933 showing an early
attempt at streamlining. This is an example of the
Mandator six cylinder petrol or diesel engined model for
up to 7½ tons payload. In this case it carries a 1,500
gallon petrol tank. Since running experimental diesel
engined vehicles from 1928, AEC had offered a six
cylinder unit as an option to their petrol engines since
1930, and a four cylinder version for the Mercury, Monarch
and Matador from 1933.

A 3 to 4 ton Guy Vixen of 1934 fitted with a Dorman Ricardo diesel engine. The Wolf 2 to 3 ton chassis and the Vixen were Guy's staple products from 1933 and 1934 respectively, until joined by the 4½ ton Otter in 1935. These and most of Guy's other less successful goods models were phased out in 1936 in favour of the Ant lightweight military model. Except when diesel powered, the majority of these Thirties' models had petrol engines made in the adjoining Henry Meadows' factory at Wolverhampton.

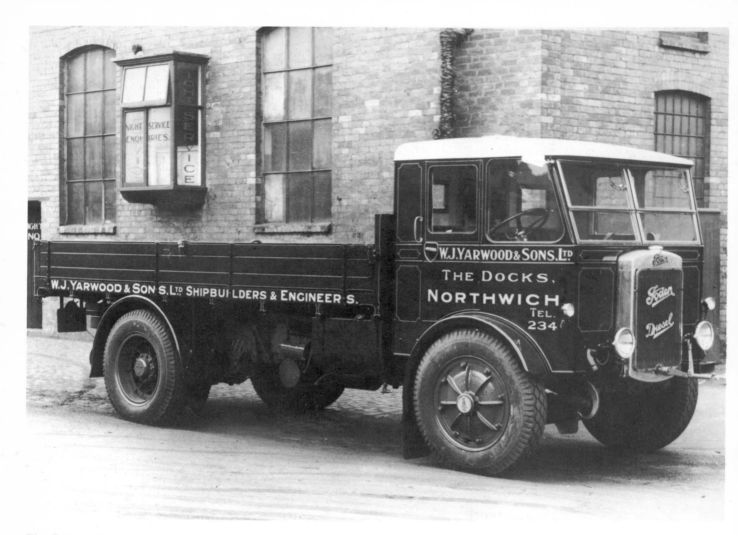

The Foden diesel had changed considerably in appearance since the pioneer 1931 model. This is a Gardner engined 6 tonner of 1933 photographed before it had been registered and taxed.

In 1935 the appearance of the Foden range was once more completely changed when streamlined cabs with steeply raked screens were fitted. At the same time five speed gearboxes became optional to improve fuel economy. Note the special wheels based on Foden's steam lorry experience in which the detachable rims are retained by bolts and clips.

Foden's six wheelers of the 1932-5 period were closely related to their heavy four wheel models. In common with other maximum capacity six wheelers of the time, their heavy build enabled them to carry only 10-12 tons within the legal 18 ton gross weight limit of their class. In fact they had strength to cope with heavier weights which allowed them to survive arduous use, notably off-road tipping, for longer than otherwise possible. In 1935 the Foden six wheelers were joined by a new rigid eight wheeler 15 ton model.

A popular way of increasing the payload space of the cheaper chassis was to have them converted to forward control. This vehicle started life as a bonneted 2 ton Bedford in 1932 but was converted before delivery to give it more body area. This allowed it to take full advantage of Bedford's guarantee that their vehicles could safely carry a 50 per cent overload. In 1933 Bedford introduced a genuine 3 ton model weighing under 2½ tons to take advantage of the £30/30 mph allowed for this class from 1 January 1934.

The original type of Gardner-Pagefield was in 1932 revised with forward control as the Pompian and at the same time this heavier Pathfinder model appeared. It was for 6 to 7 ton loads and could have either the five or six cylinder Gardner LW engine fitted. Pagefield were quite successful in the maximum capacity four and six wheel fields through the 1930s though, after the World War II, they concentrated on their lighter municipal models. Like the Armstrong-Saurer, the heaviest models were available with splitter gears to give eight forward ratios.

The Hippo was one of the Leyland T range which first appeared in 1929. This example was built in 1932 or 1933 and used for long distance trunk operation between the Lancashire textile area and London. From 1931 Leyland heavy models had been available with the firm's own six cylinder diesel engine, though it was not until 1933 that this seriously entered production and was joined by a small six for the Cub range, and by a four cylinder unit for the medium models like the Badger.

A type of vehicle which has generally fallen out of favour, except for very heavy haulage, is the road tractor. However, in the Thirties there was a considerable demand for vehicles able to tow drawbar trailers of the type often used with steam tractors in the Twenties. The Latil Traulier from France was one of the most successful and was assembled through much of the Thirties in Britain by S & D. It was unusual in having four wheel steering as well as four wheel drive and could easily handle payloads of from 10 to 15 tons. Later its principal use was in off-road timber haulage.

Left One of the heavy duty P range of 6 ton Albions is this 1933 model. Albion announced their own diesel engine option for the first time that year and were also willing to fit Dorman, Gardner and Beardmore diesels. The latter choice was unusual, though perhaps explained by both Albion and Beardmore being based in Glasgow. The example shown is interesting in being fitted with one of the earliest varieties of self-loading crane. A feature of the time was the set-forward engine and radiator to transfer weight away from the back axle, which by law was limited to a maximum of 8 tons.

Below This 1931 Scammell articulated eight wheeler has apparently changed little in outward appearance from the original 1922 model. However, apart from its lack of front wheel brakes and the provision of chain drive, it is in fact fully up to 1930s' standards with its enclosed cab, giant pneumatic tyres (Scammell favoured extra large singles) and a Gardner 6LW diesel under the bonnet. This type of Scammell, culminating in the Highwayman range of 1958, was to remain surprisingly little altered for over forty years.

The Leyland Cub marked Leyland's re-entry into the light vehicle class in 1931. Though it was initially a 2 tonner it was soon available in several heavier versions, of which a 3 ton model of 1934 is shown. It was available with six cylinder petrol or diesel engines and a four cylinder unit could be specified for town work, where extra power was unnecessary. Around 8,000 Cubs were made in just under ten years, though from 1937 sales were concentrated on a similar but lighter unladen weight Lynx model.

O'BRIEN THOMAS & CO. LTD.

Manufacturers of
The Effingham Hot Brick Cooker
The Marvel Cooker
The Wizard Boiler. Etc. Etc.

LONDON and ROTHERHAM

BAYLEYS. LTD
MAKERS
NEWINGTON CAUSEWAY, S.E.

From relatively small production in the Twenties Commer were very much more successful in the next decade following their purchase by Rootes. Their new designs were principally for the competitive 30 cwt to 3 ton market, of which this is an example of the heaviest 1934 B3 model, with bodywork by Bayleys. It could have a six cylinder petrol or four cylinder Perkins diesel engine and cost much the same as the mass-produced equivalent models from Bedford and Morris-Commercial. All the medium capacity models were replaced in 1935 by the new N range.

Above left The 3 ton Bedford, which appeared in 1933, made an enormous impact on medium weight haulage in the Thirties. It continued to cater for a 50 per cent overload with the manufacturer's approval, so was one of the highest capacity vehicles available for its price. The example shown is a 1934 model with its standard 27 hp six cylinder petrol engine replaced by a Dorman-Ricardo diesel. This was a fairly regular occurrence if cheap chassis were run for big mileages, as the cost of replacing the engine when it was in need of a major overhaul was more than made up for by fuel savings.

Far left The early Thirties Armstrong-Saurer Dominant six wheeler was a vast 11 to 12 ton capacity machine. It had a 120 bhp six cylinder diesel and four speed gearbox with splitter gear to double the number of available ratios. The petrol engined Armstrong-Saurers were discontinued in 1933, when forward control became optional on all models and a successful effort was made to reduce the excessive unladen weight of the earlier models.

Above Probably the most famous of the new class of diesel engined eight wheelers was the AEC Mammoth Major 8 which first appeared in 1934. For more conservative operators it could also be fitted with the old 120 bhp six cylinder AEC petrol engine, which gave a weight saving of 7 cwt. It had a five forward speed gearbox and, in common with many of its contemporaries, brakes on only three of its four axles. The example shown was described as the largest travelling bill board in the country. It was also one of the largest trunk vehicles with a capacity of almost 15 tons.

Dennis were very successful with their medium weight models in the Thirties. In 1933 they had introduced the 40/45 cwt range which featured set back front axles to give equal tyre loading. In normal control form its unusual appearance earned it the nickname of Flying Pig. In 1934 it became available as a trailing axle six wheeler for 3½ ton loads and at the same time was joined by the model shown, also for 3½ tons but called the 70 cwt to avoid confusion. Its short wheelbase and good steering lock made it exceptionally manoeuvrable and it was popular for municipal duties.

It is difficult to believe that this is virtually the same chassis as the adjoining forward control 70 cwt Dennis. Note the opening windscreen, a common hangover from the days before windscreen wipers in the Twenties. The cab is a semi-standardised one to help oil companies comply with petroleum regulations and includes wire mesh glass at the rear and a fuel supply isolation switch.

This type of Dennis was most commonly seen with refuse collection body or gully emptying tank.

In 1933 Maudslay introduced their Six-Four model, so called because it could carry 6 tons yet weighed under 4 tons for tax purposes. It remained their staple goods model through the mid Thirties and could either have Maudslay's own overhead valve petrol engine or the Gardner 4LW. The photograph shows one of a number of trials which took place before the war to test the suitability of ordinary goods models for military duties. In the case of Maudslay it led them to develop their Militant model which was used during the war for both military and civilian haulage. The Six-Four was replaced by the Mogul in 1937 which became their staple model in the Forties.

The DG range of steam Sentinels, which had been joined in 1930 by Britain's first rigid eight wheeler, the DG8, were superseded in 1933 by the highly sophisticated S range of which under 1,000 were produced. A 1935 S4 6 to 7 tonner is shown. They were available as four, six and eight wheelers and were the last major design of steam lorry to appear. Their principal changes, as compared with previous Sentinels, were a far lower unladen weight, at last comparable with diesel engined chassis, and the use of a four cylinder horizontal engine with shaft drive to the rear wheels.

Crossley were best known for their buses and cars, though during the Thirties they produced a number of military trucks and a few civilian goods models. These included the Delta petrol or diesel engined 4 tonner, the 6 ton Atlas and the 7 ton Beta. The 1935 example shown is a 12 ton six wheel version of the latter.

Following the transfer of Garner production to the Sentinel factory a new range of Sentinel Garners appeared in 1935. They continued Garner's patent hinge-out wings and could be powered by either Austin or Meadows petrol engines, or Perkins diesels. The vehicle shown is the 5 tonner which, like its smaller sisters, featured an engine mounted on rollers which could be rolled out of the front of the chassis for major repairs. Both Sentinel and Garner soon got into financial difficulties and the latter were moved to a new London factory in 1936.

The Commer N range appeared in 1935 and was a further step in the manufacturer's move towards mass-production and the ability to compete with Ford, Morris and Bedford. It was to be by far their most successful model programme and included vehicles from 1 ton payload to 5 tons. The example shown is the N5 for 4 to 5 ton loads. It had a six cylinder petrol engine and weighed under 2½ tons unladen. A smaller N4 version covered the 3 to 4 ton class.

The old established firm of Vulcan had reached a low ebb in 1935 when they supplied this 3 ton tipper to a London building contactor. Their speciality was light commercial and small wheeled municipal chassis in the 30 cwt to 4 ton class and they were feeling fierce competition from cheaper mass-produced vehicles. In 1938 the company was bought by Tilling-Stevens.

Below The Leyland Cub started life in 1931 as a quality-built six cylinder 2 tonner. It was given an optional four cylinder petrol engine in 1932 and a six cylinder diesel in 1933. To avoid direct competition with the far cheaper products of Ford, Bedford and others it gradually moved up the payload scale and the example shown is a 1937 4 tonner. In that year Leyland introduced the Lynx using many Cub parts but designed to take better advantage of the concessions for vehicles weighing under 2½ tons unladen. The Lynx could carry 5 tons.

Far right A typical mid Thirties 3 ton Bedford. This model did much to expand the medium haulage market and, with its smaller sisters, had captured 40 per cent of sales in the 30 cwt/3 ton bracket by 1936. Two tons had formerly marked the upper limit of vehicles which could sell in sufficient quantities to interest the American backed mass-producers, like Ford and Bedford. Bedford, however, successfully moved this limit upwards into the medium category and forced many of the traditional makers into the heavy class, where the comparatively low sales potential was of little interest to the very large companies producing as many identical models as possible.

The Foden eight wheeler first appeared in 1935, and this is an example of the DG 6/15 model of 1937, by which time the original steeply raked screen and D-fronted cab of the initial model had been redesigned.

In 1929, following their first undertype in 1926, Foden had, like Sentinel, developed a final advanced steam range – the Speed Six and Twelve undertypes – but these had been superseded by the diesel models after 1932. Foden were the last of the steam lorry firms to make the successful change to diesel. Many of the others tried and failed, including Sentinel after the war.

The Guy Vixen was a similar concept to the Leyland Cub, being a medium capacity vehicle, in this case for 3 tons. It provided longer life than the contemporary mass-produced vehicle, but was more expensive. Like the Cub it was available with forward or normal control and with diesel or petrol engine, two choices only available on some of the mass-produced vehicles.

Though the Vixen was most common with forward control, its protruberant bonneted layout and set-back front wheels made engine maintenance particularly easy. It also helped to spread the load between the two axles, avoiding overloading and improving tyre and brake life.

The 7V range announced by Ford in 1937 marked their first serious move into the heavier truck class. The 3 and 5 ton examples could use either a 30 hp V8 petrol engine or, for more conservative and cost-conscious operators, a 24 hp four cylinder engine. Like nearly all the other American-backed truck firms in Britain, diesels were not offered before World War II. This example is equipped with a tank for normal municipal work but it could be quickly converted in the event of an air raid for fire fighting and gas decontamination purposes.

Like Ford, Dodges in the Thirties were usually British assembled and designed. This is the standard 2 ton Luton van which cost £306 complete in 1937. Larger Dodges of the time included 3, 4 and 4/5 ton models which had similar styling to the example shown but a shorter bonnet made possible by positioning the engine partially in the cab. The largest Dodges were popular as tippers and a similar chassis was available as the basis of a 10 ton articulated outfit.

The Scammell rigid eight wheeler appeared in prototype form in 1935 and soon adopted this styling, which it retained for almost twenty-five years. It featured Scammell's own four cylinder petrol engine, or the Gardner 6LW diesel engine, and had a single driven axle at the rear, as shown in this photograph by the large hub cap hiding the bolts retaining its half shaft. It had an epicyclic double-reduction axle, a six speed gearbox and, most unusually, rubber suspension on the rear bogie. Single tyres all round kept its weight to the minimum.

The Morris-Commercial Equi-Load (approximately equal loading on each tyre) or CV range of 30 cwt to 5 ton models replaced the C range in 1937. In the next two years over 12,500 were sold and a small number were produced during the war for essential purposes. Shortly before the war Morris decided to build their own diesel engine. This was an unusual step for a mass producer of commercial vehicles as all had relied on buying proprietary diesels to instal in their chassis for the relatively few operators who could see any advantage in having expensive engines in cheap, short life chassis. Morris realised that the fuel cost advantage of the diesel in cheap medium weight trucks would be an added sales attraction if they could reduce its manufacturing costs sufficiently. A few diesel engines were produced under licence from Saurer, following Armstrong-Saurer's withdrawal from lorry manufacture, but the war delayed their introduction until the later Forties. However even then they were well ahead of Ford, Austin, Commer, Dodge and Bedford who chiefly used well proven Perkins engines when asked to supply diesel vehicles.

An important newcomer in 1938 was the Seddon 6 tonner, one of the largest diesel vehicles to weigh under 2½ tons and, therefore, qualify for 30 mph running. It was built by the garage and haulage firm of Foster and Seddon in Oldham around the well-tried Perkins P6 engine. About twenty were made up to 1940, with a further sixty early in the war. After the war, Seddon were to become major manufacturers of diesel trucks and were one of the last new manufacturers to attain long-term commercial success.

Following their departure from the Sentinel waggon works, Garner bought a new factory in North London and resumed production in 1936. They soon designed a range of very stylish new models but only the 3 and 4/5 ton versions ever entered production. They were first available in 1937 and the 4/5 ton example shown here dates from 1938. At the same time development work was taking place on 4 x 4 army lorries, which soon replaced the civilian models. After the war chassis were no longer produced, though the company still makes bodywork.

Right The twin-steer six wheeler became a popular configuration from its adoption by ERF and Foden in 1937. This is the aptly named Leyland Steer of 1938. The twin-steer, sometimes called Chinese Six, had the advantage of a lower unladen weight than normal six wheelers, especially ones with double-drive bogeys and twin wheels on both rear axles.

Below The appearance of the Bedford was revised in 1938 and now featured the familiar rounded radiator illustrated. Though the largest model was still only a 3 tonner, several were fitted with the Scammell automatic trailer coupling and trailer, which doubled the payload capacity. This had first been used on the Scammell mechanical horse. These Bedford-Scammells were a popular model for many years.

Apart from their appearance the WL and WH 2 ton and WTL and WTH semi-forward control 3 ton models were mechanically similar to their predecessors and used 27 hp six cylinder petrol engines.

Though the Lynx had virtually replaced the Cub in 1937 a few lightweight 6 ton six wheel Cubs were produced up to the war. The Cub had grown up considerably since appearing as a 2 tonner in 1931.

The petroleum regulations of the Twenties were now less complicated though, as can be seen, the exhaust system was kept well forward of the load space. Note the electric semaphore direction indicators adopted by many commercial vehicles in the mid Thirties.

A 1938 Thornycroft Sturdy tipper. Despite its name it was in fact
built to weigh under 2½ tons unladen and therefore work at
30 mph. The Sturdy range then included 4 to 6 ton models with
forward or normal control and all had Thornycroft 3.9 litre 60
bhp petrol engines, shared with the smaller Nippy 3 tonner.

Commer's N range was replaced in 1939 by the Q range or Superpoise. Like the contemporary Morris-Commercial Equiload, this name signified the balance between front and back axles made possible by engine and front axle positioning and the short bonnet.

The Superpoise range covered 1½ to 6 tons payload capacity and could be fitted with six cylinder petrol or Perkins diesel engines. The example shown is a 2/3 ton Superpoise in use in Scotland. The Superpoise with various styling changes remained in production for over twenty years.

Right A 1939 twin-steer DG model Foden seen in service some ten years after it first left the factory. Like all Fodens of the late Thirties it was powered by a Gardner diesel engine.

Below This Leyland Beaver epitomises the heavy four wheel goods vehicle of the late Thirties and was one of the most popular models. The example shown was made in 1939 and could legally carry about 7¼ tons. Beavers were available with four or six cylinder petrol or diesel engines of 65 to 104 bhp. Though this sounds a low output by today's standards it was quite adequate for the 20 mph legal limit still in force.

Left Because of their low price and durability a number of quantity-produced American vehicles were sold in Britain in the late Thirties. They included GMC, Indiana, White, Reo, certain Fords, and the International shown here, an articulated 1939 model. With civilian vehicle shortages during the war a number of similar vehicles were supplied to Britain under the Lend-Lease scheme.

Below A surprise newcomer to the medium weight commercial vehicle scene in 1939 was Austin. They had made lorries during and immediately after World War I, but since then had concentrated on cars and car-based light commercials. However, their 1939 range comprised 30 cwt, 2 ton and 3 ton models using 3460 cc overhead valve petrol engines. Several thousand including the 3 tonner shown were supplied during the war. Note its lamp masks for blackout driving and the white edges to its wings and bumper to improve visibility.

Left By the outbreak of war, about fifty Atkinson diesel lorries had been built, as four, six and, from 1937, eight wheelers, mostly with Gardner engines. During the war Atkinson made six and eight wheelers with Gardner and AEC diesels.

Between 1931 and reformation in 1933, Atkinson had made a few Blackstone and Dorman diesel engined vehicles using remnants of their steam lorries.

Below World War II brought an urgent need to step up vehicle production. To achieve this many of the styling refinements of the Thirties were omitted.

This is a 3 ton Bedford simplified. During the hostilities, around a quarter of a million Bedfords were produced for civilian and military transport. This example is shown working in 1941 for the Pool Board who controlled the supply of all motor fuel in the country.

A 70 cwt Dennis of 1939 has its capacity increased to 6 tons by the Scammell articulated semi-trailer. It has a 3.77 litre four cylinder Dennis petrol engine. A larger rigid version of the same model using the same engine was developed in 1939 for the 2½ ton/30 mph category. Like the Seddon it could just carry 6 tons if suitably lightweight bodywork was used. After the war this model re-emerged as the Pax.

An example of the Dennis Max showing the austerity pattern cab
fitted through most of the war to save manufacturing time.
The Max had been introduced in 1937 to carry the greatest
possible payload under the 12 ton legal limit on two axles. It
weighed only 3 tons 8½ cwt, allowing 8 tons to be carried on a
lightweight platform. It could have Dennis' new 04 diesel
engine, or a petrol unit, and a five speed gearbox giving
clutchless changes into overdrive top.

Preservation Scene

The heavy vehicle preservation movement got off to a far slower and far later start than its veteran and vintage car counterparts. The first rally, at Beaulieu, was not held until 1957, and the Historic Commercial Vehicle Club only came into being a year later.

However, from the handful of members in the early days, it has now grown to several thousand, with a comparable increase in public interest. After all, old lorries, buses, fire engines, steamers, and other types of special purpose commercial vehicles often make a far more spectacular and colourful sight than a group of contemporary old cars.

Most summer weekends will find 50,000 or more enthusiasts and their families attending rallies all over the country, and such road runs as the HCVC London-Brighton on the first Sunday each May attract 200 entries and a million or so spectators.

For various reasons 1919-1939 (or vintage) commercial vehicles of over 3 ton capacity are surprisingly scarce, both compared with their lighter sisters and with cars. This is partly due to the lack of interest in preserving them before even the youngest was twenty years old, and the fact that they were normally too big to be quietly forgotten by their original owners in the barns and sheds where many cars and vans have survived intact. Then again, they had a far harder working life than lighter vehicles, and did a far greater mileage. As if these points were not enough to have imperilled their survival, there is still another far more significant reason – their great weight and therefore high scrap value, particularly during World War II when home produced metal was so vital. Ironically, it has been scrapyards that have provided the majority of preserved commercial vehicles because, luckily, many of these are run in such a haphazard way that the first vehicles in are the last to be cut up. Even now an overgrown yard with piles of modern wrecks near the entrance will reveal remarkable historic relics in the back reaches – relics which sadly will often be impossible to extract before they disintegrate entirely.

Because the British climate is so damaging to vehicles left in the open, a great many of the preserved lorries have had to be rebuilt, using other survivors or rotten remains as patterns. This has meant that there are very few early commercials looking exactly as they would have done when actually working for a living. Unfortunately, this lack of authenticity is aggravated by modern owners not sticking to the original livery of their vehicles, which are often painted in over-strong colours and spoiled by the effect of too flamboyant lining-out and lettering, and too garish lamps and accessories more suited to luxury cars. Sadly the genuine 'feel' of some of these vehicles is lost by the desire of certain owners to publicise their business with anachronistic painted references to TV maintenance, or caravan hire, or perhaps crash repairs, in modern style lettering. Another unfortunate lapse is when the owner screws rally attendance plaques to his cab or dashboard. However, 'it's a free country', and future generations should at least be pleased that this important segment of motoring and industrial history has not been forgotten, and that at any rate some owners have made great efforts to keep strictly to the original.

One problem which faces the owners of the 250 or so preserved heavy commercials is the alarmingly increased cost of restoring them and then running them. To have parts made is beyond the reach of most owners, so that a considerable degree of ingenuity often has to be used to get round mechanical problems. Though many bemoan the way in which values of commercial vehicles have rocketed now that enthusiasts appreciate their scarcity, and the enjoyment to be gained from driving them, at least it bears some comparison with the increased preservation costs. This will mean that, with luck, enthusiasts will be encouraged to tackle the dozens of incomplete or badly weathered commercials still to be found, or already awaiting restoration in collectors' hands, so that new and unique Twenties and Thirties vehicles should still be taking to the road again for many years to come. This is particularly important as some of the remaining projects are the sole survivors of once important makes which might otherwise be all but forgotten.

How a few vintage heavy commercial vehicles ended their days if they were lucky enough to avoid being cut up as soon as they were scrapped. Contrast this picture with the same lorry on the front cover for, in fact, they are the same vehicle.

The Caledon was rescued from the Lake District where it had been the base of a homemade house. Over the years it had become more and more tumble-down and was on the verge of being scrapped when rescued by the author and carefully restored over four years to original condition.

BRITISH MAKERS OF HEAVY GOODS VEHICLES ABLE TO CARRY 3 TONS AND UPWARDS AND AVAILABLE BETWEEN 1919 AND 1939

Where the manufacturer only existed for some of the period, approximate starting and/or finishing dates are given. In this context light vehicles are taken to carry under 3 tons; medium from 3 to 5 tons; and heavy, anything above and up to the normal legal maximum of 22 tons gross.

ADC.
(Associated Daimler) Southall. For two years, from 1926, the products of AEC and Daimler were jointly marketed under this name. They then separated and Daimler concentrated on buses and coaches, as well as cars.

AEC.
Southall. One of the biggest manufacturers of the period. Principally known for its London buses, but its World War I army lorries were widely used in civilian haulage for many years. Made light and medium trucks in the Twenties, and were the first to make their own diesel engine in 1928 (offered to the public in 1930). Concentrated on medium and heavy models in the Thirties, including the famous Mammoth, Majestic, Matador, Monarch, Mercury etc. introduced in the late Twenties. The well known Mammoth Major eight wheeler appeared in 1934.

AJS.
Wolverhampton. In 1929 and 1930, made a few bus and coach chassis which were also available for goods transport.

Albion.
Glasgow. Scotland's principal maker of light, medium and heavy commercial vehicles. Its chain drive World War I 3 ton trucks were used for many years in civilian haulage. Made some of the earliest six wheelers for normal as opposed to military haulage, in the late Twenties. Produced eight wheelers from 1937.

Allchin.
Northampton. Built a few primitive steam waggons in the Twenties.

Armstrong-Saurer.
Scotswood-on-Tyne. Armstrong-Whitworth made Swiss Saurers under licence between 1931 and 1937. Very popular particularly with diesel engines, in the maximum capacity four, six and eight wheel market.

Arran.
Welwyn Garden City. Produced a few medium capacity forward control trucks 1934-6.

Atkinson.
Preston. Important steam waggon maker in the Twenties. Produced a few diesel heavy lorries from 1931, and was reformed in 1933 to concentrate on diesels, approximately fifty being produced before World War II.

Austin.
Birmingham. Made army lorries 1914-18, but then concentrated on cars and light vehicles until entering the medium field in 1939.

Aveling.
Rochester. Built a few steam waggons in the Twenties.

Bean.
Tipton. Was important light vehicle maker, but also produced a few 4 tonners before going bankrupt in 1932.

Beardmore Multiwheeler.
London. Around 1930, light vehicle maker Beardmore assembled French Chenard et Walcker road tractors similar to Scammells. These heavy vehicles were later made by a separate company called Multiwheeler.

Belhaven.
Wishaw. Small Scottish maker of medium trucks up to 1930.
Bell.
Manchester. A maker of light trucks for the Co-operative movement between 1922 and 1929; also produced a few 6 tonners in 1920.
Bedford.
Luton. Introduced as an anglicised replacement for the 2 ton Chevrolet in 1931, the Bedford soon moved into the medium weight range and became the highest selling make. Often used as the basis for six wheel conversions either with an extra rear axle or as an articulated outfit.
Belsize.
Manchester. A well known early manufacturer which had collapsed by the mid Twenties.
Bristol.
Bristol. Best known for buses and coaches but also made approximately 650 4 ton chassis used both for trucks and buses in the Twenties.
British Ensign.
London. Quite successful lorry maker during World War I, but collapsed in the slump which followed.
Brotherhood.
Peterborough. In about 1920, built a few steam waggons similar in appearance to Yorkshire with transverse boiler.
Burford.
London. Originally made in America by Fremont-Mais and sold by H. G. Burford. Became increasingly English in content during the Twenties and concentrated on light to medium and off-road trucks until 1935. Associated with Lacre latterly.
Burrell.
Thetford. Produced a few steam waggons in the Twenties.
Caledon.
Glasgow. From 1919, made 200-300 medium and heavy trucks before bankruptcy in 1926. Possibly built the first production British rigid six wheeler in 1924, a 10-12 tonner. Bought by Garrett in 1927.
Carrimore.
London. Articulated trailer maker who also for a few years from 1929 produced tractor portion for up to 17 tons payload.
Churchill.
Sheffield. Made a few medium commercials, principally for passenger work, up to 1925.
Clarkson.
Chelmsford. Until mid Twenties, made 3-4 ton steam chassis principally for passenger work.
Clayton.
Lincoln. Produced a few steam waggons during the Twenties.
Clyde.
Wishaw. Was a small Scottish maker of light and medium trucks until the mid Thirties.
Commer.
Luton. A major manufacturer of light and medium trucks, particularly after acquisition in 1928 by Rootes Brothers, who turned it from traditional methods to mass production in order to compete with Ford, Bedford, Morris etc. during the Thirties. Made smallest diesel trucks of their day in 1933.
County.
Manchester. A World War I 3-4 ton truck manufacturer who survived for a year or two afterwards.
Crossley.
Manchester. Produced mainly coaches, buses and light military trucks, but became moderately important for medium and heavy trucks during the Thirties.
Daimler.
Coventry. Their World War I 3 ton chassis continued to serve civilian hauliers for many years. However, from 1919 Daimler concentrated on passenger vehicles and a few light goods chassis. *See also* ADC.

Dearne.
Barnsley. Built a few 3 tonners around 1930.
Dennis.
Guildford. A major manufacturer in all but the lightest weight categories, though during the Thirties concentrated on medium models, and was not particularly successful with the heavier Max and six wheel Max Major. Unlike comparable companies, did not enter the eight wheel market. Very successful in the municipal and fire engine fields.
Dodge.
Kew. Successful in the light field, but did not produce medium vehicles until the mid Thirties.
Easyloader.
London. Built small wheeled 3 ton freighter similar to S & D in late Twenties and early Thirties.
Electricar.
Birmingham. Unlike most electric vehicles, which were for light payloads, Electricar made medium and heavy models in the Twenties and Thirties, some even as rigid six wheelers.
ERF.
Sandbach. E. R. Foden was a member of the Foden family. In 1933 he started his own company to make medium and heavy diesel-engined trucks. Six wheelers produced from 1934, and eight wheelers from 1935. First twin-steer six wheeler in 1937.
Foden.
Sandbach. Famed for steam waggons which stuck to locomotive as opposed to vertical boilers longer than virtually all their contemporaries. Foden entered the diesel medium/heavy market in 1931 and soon afterwards abandoned steam. Made 15½ ton eight wheelers from 1935, and twin-steer six wheelers from late 1937.
Ford.
Dagenham. All Ford's vehicles in Britain in the Twenties fall below our 3 ton limit. However, several were converted to rigid or articulated six wheelers from the mid Thirties, and the 1937 7V

range with four cylinder or V8 petrol engines could carry 3 to 5 tons. From 1939 the heavier British built examples were sold as Thames.
Foster.
Lincoln. Made a few steam waggons in the early Twenties.
Fowler.
Leeds. Following steam waggons, Fowler built a small number of medium and heavy diesel trucks in the first half of the 1930s.
FWD.
Slough. An American make which became famous for its 4 x 4 go-anywhere qualities in World War I. Afterwards, a firm in Slough specialised in reconditioning them and, as American parts ran out, substituted local ones until it became a wholly British product. Also made 6 x 6 versions for 6 ton loads after 1927. Name changed to Hardy soon after acquisition by AEC in 1929, in order to avoid confusion with the still active American company.
Garner.
Birmingham (later Shrewsbury, then London). Like Burford, started as an American vehicle which was made from English parts after 1924, and was popular in the medium weight range. Joined forces with Sentinel in the early Thirties, but later became independent and moved to London. Haulage models abandoned in 1939 in favour of 4 x 4 military 3 tonners.
Garrett.
Leiston. Primarily steam and electric vehicles but following takeover of Caledon in 1927 made a few petrol and, soon afterwards, diesel lorries, the latter being the first to be made in Britain in 1928.
Gilford.
London and High Wycombe. Produced successful light high-speed goods and passenger chassis with high proportion of American parts including most engines. Made medium trucks from 1930 until 1936, but principally important for coaches.

Guy.

Wolverhampton. Built mainly under 2½ tonners and light military six wheelers in the Twenties. However moved into medium category in 1928 and also made a few heavy Goliath six wheelers around 1930. Principally important in the Thirties for Wolf, Vixen and Otter light and medium models. *See also* Star.

Halley.

Glasgow. Second only to Albion in importance in Scotland. Unusual in offering six cylinder engines from 1919, ten years before they became general practice in heavy vehicles. Made most categories of goods vehicles up to end of business in 1935.

Hallford.

Dartford. Famous early make based on Saurer but never regained position after World War I, and stopped vehicle production in 1925.

Hardy.

Slough. Associated with FWD and succeeded them as AEC subsidiary responsible for all-wheel drive vehicles in the 1930s.

HSG.

London. In the old Gilford works, made a few trucks able to run on producer gas. Transferred to Sentinel and discontinued in 1938.

Jensen.

West Bromwich. From 1937 Jensen experimented, for road tax and legal speed reasons, with the lightest possible vehicle able to carry the maximum possible payload. They produced a number of integral aluminium 6 tonners weighing under 2½ tons and permitted to travel at 30 mph.

Karrier.

Huddersfield (Luton from 1934). An important medium and heavy vehicle maker who developed a useful sideline in municipal vehicles and mechanical horses, and also specialised in a wide range of rigid six wheelers from 1927. Joined forces with Commer in 1934 following takeover by Rootes.

Kerr Stuart.

Stoke-on-Trent. A pioneer British diesel lorry maker, who produced a few McLaren-Benz engined vehicles in 1929/30.

Lacre.

Letchworth. A successful early maker who produced medium but old-fashioned trucks through the Twenties and finally concentrated on a successful sideline – roadsweepers. Controlled Burford in late Twenties and early Thirties.

Liberty.

London. Like FWD and Peerless, this was a successful type of American World War I truck. They were reconditioned afterwards and a few new ones built from spares, including rigid six wheelers in the early Thirties. Later ones had diesel engines.

Latil.

Letchworth. A French make notable for front wheel drive and lowloading height in the Twenties. In the Thirties a 4 x 4 and four wheel steer road or cross-country tractor was assembled in Britain by S & D similar to later Unipower, and popular for heavy haulage.

Leyland.

Leyland. Probably the largest medium and heavy truck manufacturer of the period, and certainly on a par with AEC, Dennis, Thornycroft and Albion. Made a few steam waggons until disposing of division to Atkinson in 1926. Their famous World War I RAF types were reconditioned by the company during the Twenties, and were the backbone of many fleets for two decades. Very successful in the medium and heavy markets of the Thirties with such models as Cub, Badger, Beaver, Bison, Bull, Hippo, and, from 1934, the Octopus eight wheeler.

Mann.

Leeds. Was a fairly successful steam waggon maker until the late Twenties.

Maudslay.

Coventry. Another famous 3 ton truck supplier to

the 1914-18 War Department. Afterwards increasingly moved into bus and coach field, but always offered medium and heavy goods chassis though production often under 100 per year. Unusual in having overhead camshaft petrol engines.

McCurd.
Slough. A small manufacturer of medium trucks who survived until about 1927.

Morris-Commercial.
Birmingham. Very important in the 30-50 cwt market in the Twenties, but did not introduce medium models until 1929 with the Leader, followed by the unsuccessful Courier. Redesigned medium models in 1933 as the C range. These were replaced by CV Equiload in 1937 for up to 6 tons.

Multiwheelers.
London. The successor to Beardmore Multiwheelers. Produced a few heavy articulated or drawbar tractor outfits in the Thirties.

Pagefield.
Wigan. Made a wide range of medium vehicles during the Twenties and in 1930 produced the first all-British diesel lorry, a Gardner engined 5 tonner. Built medium and heavy goods chassis during Thirties, plus Pagefield System (pioneer demountable-body refuse collectors).

Palladium.
London. Best known for medium trucks during World War I; had disappeared by 1926.

Peerless.
Slough. Rebuilder and reconditioner of wartime American Peerless lorries; continued to produce English equivalents in small numbers until the mid Thirties. *See also* Trader.

Ransomes.
Ipswich. Produced a few steam waggons during the Twenties.

Roebuck.
Birmingham. Was a small heavy six wheel 12 ton lorry maker 1930-4.

Robey.
Lincoln. Built a few steam waggons in the Twenties.

Scammell.
Watford. Started in 1921 to make first heavy articulated units in Britain. These were produced throughout the period plus rigids and special cross-country vehicles from 1927. Made first 100 ton heavy haulage lorry in 1929. Was renowned for three wheel mechanical horses in the Thirties.

Scammell & Nephew.
London. Originally connected with pioneer Scammell artic. before Scammell lorries moved to Watford. Mainly body builders but produced 5 ton low-loader in 1933.

Scout.
Salisbury. Was a small local manufacturer producing a few medium lorries until the early Twenties.

S & D.
Letchworth. Specialised in small-wheeled low-load manoeuvrable chassis from 1922; later popular for municipal duties. Assembled Latil in the Thirties.

Seddon.
Oldham. New in 1938, the Seddon was a 6 tonner built as lightly as possible to qualify for tax and speed concessions. Approximately twenty were built before the outbreak of war.

Sentinel.
Shrewsbury. The best known steam waggon maker; continued to produce steamers through the Twenties and Thirties even after their chief rivals Foden, Garrett and Yorkshire had switched to diesels. Made four, six and the first British eight wheeler (1930), culminating in very advanced S models in 1933. Were associated with Garner in the mid Thirties and experimented with HSG producer gas vehicles shortly before the war. These emerged afterwards in modified form as the first Sentinel diesels.

Shefflex.
Sheffield. Small maker of light lorries who, from

1930, fitted several with trailing third axles to make them suitable for up to 6 ton loads. Their 2½ ton model of 1931 was one of the smallest vehicles available with a diesel engine.

Star.
Wolverhampton. Made 3 tonners in the early Twenties. Owned by Guy from 1927 until 1932, and made light, high speed four and six cylinder goods chassis of which later models went up to 65 cwt payload.

Straker-Squire.
London. Was an important early medium vehicle maker who never regained success after World War I and disappeared in 1928.

Straussler.
London. Advanced all-wheel drive tractors and lorries in the late Thirties plus eight wheel tankers and mechanical horses. Helped design Garner 3 ton 4 x 4.

Sunbeam.
Wolverhampton. Produced goods vehicles based on bus chassis available, at least in theory, around 1931.

Tasker.
Andover. Petrol road tankers in the late Twenties and Little Giant steam vehicles.

Thornycroft.
Basingstoke. Major medium and heavy vehicle maker throughout the period, though concentrated much of energy on overseas and military markets. J model from World War I widely used in civilian transport for many years afterwards. Over 40 commercial models available by 1931. The 4 ton Sturdy of 1932 and 7½-8 ton Trusty from 1934 were well known Thirties' goods models.

Tilling-Stevens.
Maidstone. Remembered best for petrol-electric drive passenger vehicles though medium and heavy petrol-electric and gear-drive goods vehicles were produced through much of the period. Often known as TSM in the Thirties. Made unusual flat eight

cylinder diesel 8 tonner in 1937. Absorbed Vulcan in 1938.

Trader.
Slough. An offshoot of the British Peerless Company. Made medium and heavy diesel trucks during the Thirties.

Union.
London. Union Cartage Company produced Gardner engined road tractors for their own use between 1935 and 1939.

Unipower.
Perivale. Converted many popular four wheel goods models to six wheelers and from 1937 also made 4 x 4 tractors similar to Latil.

Vulcan.
Southport. Produced generally light vehicles and military six wheelers in the Twenties, though increasingly heavy diesel-engined lorries in the Thirties. Merged with Tilling-Stevens from 1938.

Wallis & Steevens.
Basingstoke. Built a few steam waggons in the Twenties.

Watson.
Newcastle-upon-Tyne. Was a small manufacturer who, through most of the Twenties, produced medium trucks for the local market.

W & G.
London. Made mainly light vehicles, but also a few 3 tonners in the early Thirties.

Yorkshire.
Leeds. Was an even longer lived steam waggon maker than Foden. Used unusual transverse boiler design. Made diesel lorries, including eight wheelers, for a time in the mid Thirties.

Many other British makes of vehicle including **Napier** and **Wolseley** dating from World War I were also still in use with operators in the Twenties. This also applied to such American vehicles as **Mack, Pierce-Arrow, Peerless, FWD, Riker, Packard,**

Liberty, USA Heavy Aviation, GMC etc. Some of these were also imported afterwards as well as Autocar, Brockway, Diamond T, Federal, Graham, Gotfredson (Canada), Indiana, International, Reo Speed Trucks (very successful in the late Twenties and Thirties), Republic, etc.

Numerous European makes were also offered in Britain during the period, but few sold in any quantity. Some of the best known were: Auto Traction (Belgium); Berliet (France); Berna (Switzerland, but also assembled in Britain during World War I); Fiat (Italy); Laffly (France – mainly municipal vehicles); Mercedes-Benz (Germany – first diesel lorry available in Britain in 1927); Lancia (Italy – mainly passenger service vehicles); Minerva (Belgium – took over Auto Traction who made articulated vehicles similar to Scammell); Renault (France); and Saurer (Switzerland – supplied diesels to Britain in the late Twenties following considerable success with their high quality petrol vehicles there earlier).

INDEX TO HEAVY VEHICLE MAKERS